My Sister and Brother Helped Me Heal:

From Broken to Whole

Visionary: Dr. Chavon Anette

Copyright

Copyright © 2023 by Chavon Thomas

Cover Design: iambiancabrown.com

Printed in the USA:
All rights reserved. No part of this book may be reproduced or used in any manner without the written permission of the copyright owner except for the use of quotations in a book review.

For more information, address: www.chavonanette.com

Dedication

To the Power and Grace Leaders Movement Family and My Sister and Brother Helped Me Heal Family

Table of Contents

Foreword
by Dr. Heather Kinchlow — i

Chapter 1
My Cluster Blessed My Womb by Jess Simmons — 1

Chapter 2
Accept Whom God Sends by Rev. Shelia K. Cook — 7

Chapter 3
Buried Addiction by By Jarius Hillman — 13

Chapter 4
The Bridge by Prophetess Adrianne Demauchet — 19

Chapter 5
As I waited Patiently, My Brother Helped Me Heal by Elder Kerry Freeman — 25

Chapter 6
Not My Own by Paige Edmonds — 33

Chapter 7
Shed to Soar by Prophetess Ronjeanna Harris — 41

Epilogue
Destiny Helpers by Dr. Chavon Anette — 49

Foreword

Dr. Heather Kinchlow

Dr. Chavon Annette is an emerging 21st-century leader, forging a path that equips individuals toward their true destiny. For over a decade, I have watched her become an extraordinary author, coach, and business leader. I am in awe of her growth and have been encouraged by her tenacity to soar above disappointment, pain, and setbacks. Despite her defeats, she remains committed to building her faith, growing in wisdom, and supporting others. Through her anthology, *My Sister Helped Me Heal*, Chavon created a safe space for women sisters to be real. We are all learning to uncover the unique treasures within each other, often buried in shame, pain, and tears forged through vicissitudes. Those who once felt hopeless become beacons of hope, light, and purpose through an unbreakable bond of sisterhood that she has established.

No matter how painful or horrific the years are, Chavon masterfully helps each individual recognize the benefits of their life journey. Throughout this book, *My Sister Helped Me Heal*, the themes resonate as a compilation of real life and a compelling display of triumph during difficult times. As you read these pages, embark on a journey with our sisters, those willing to share truths usually hidden and kept secret. Despite all the destruction, I admired every sister willing to take the time to help us feel and heal again. They allowed us to cry and accept a greater calling and purpose. Your life will never be the same again. This is because you will meet real sisters within these pages that linked arms together and challenged one another to stand within our worth and dominion. This is a daily choice to accept how God truly sees you.

Perceptiveness is everything. We pray that you begin to awaken through your sister's messages and no longer need to wait for someone else to validate your regal identity. Embrace your greatness, and permit yourself to soar above the lies, pain, and internal negative voices. This book is only the beginning. An abundant, unlimited lifestyle is available in every area of your life. It is inside of you right now. Dr. Chavon Annette and her sisters have taken the time to water your seeds of greatness as you navigate your next steps. Your capacity for the best mental and physical health, wealth, relationships, and faith in God is limitless. Meditate on these truths, receive them as your new paradigm, honor God and yourself while serving others, then watch unimaginable change occur.

DR. HEATHER KINCHLOW,
EXECUTIVE COACH & NEUROPLASTIC - THERAPIST,
FOUNDER OF THE MIND BRAIN ACADEMY & PRAYER SCHOOL GLOBAL

Chapter 1

My Cluster Blessed My Womb

Jess Simmons

I remember sitting in our bathroom waiting for the two lines to appear on our 144,852,669 pregnancy test. I waited the entire two weeks; I had all the symptoms, and I felt weird. This had to be the moment! My husband and I have been actively trying to conceive for at least two years. Through the doctor's appointments, medications, consultations, shots, and miscarriages, I secretly lost hope but remained hopeful and optimistic for my husband. Once the timer went off, I picked up the test, and once again, there was one bold line on my EPT Pregnancy test indicating that we would have to endure yet another month of trying to conceive what God promised me.

You see, I was told after the birth of my son that I would no longer be able to conceive due to medical issues from my previous pregnancy. However, one day, while sitting at work, I heard God say, "You shall carry in your womb and deliver again. I, the Lord, will make it happen." So, month after month, I questioned God on how they could make me a promise and endure the pain of waiting for it to pass. Witnessing my close friends announce their pregnancies, attending gender reveals and baby showers, being asked to be a new god mommy to a baby that I helped pray for their mother through their conception, and still, I had to wait for God to bless my womb.

My womb was already blessed. There were no issues with my reproductive system; all my reproductive organs were healthy and whole, and my lab work always showed normal values, yet I still chose to focus on what I thought I lacked. On our last negative test day, I decided to surrender all my planning, timing my ovulation, recording my temperatures, and altering my lifestyle to God and hold Him to His word. I forgot that God is a keeper of His word, and if He has declared a thing, it will happen.

As I continued living in expectation of the promise, I consciously traded in my garment of hurt, embarrassment, and frustration and put on my garment of praise. Throughout my infertility journey, I had to give God a complete yes to bear the hard days and sad moments and remember that God still had me on His mind. I served in every capacity that I could: within my local church, in sister ministries, and in the community, and I even started my own women's Ministry, Peculiar Pearls.

At the ministry's launch, I hosted a luncheon to raise money for a woman of God diagnosed with Breast Cancer. All the proceeds went to her, and other ladies blessed her. We shared so much love and empowerment that day, but the nugget that stuck out to me the most was that pearls grow in clusters! After a beautiful afternoon, I asked Prophetess Gayle to close us out in prayer. We formed a circle and called on God together, and then she came to me, placed her hand on my stomach, and said, "God has blessed your womb with you and your husband's heart desires. She will be a mighty warrior for God, and you will have a healthy and safe pregnancy." All I could do was weep. Who would have ever thought that my being a conduit of bringing people together to be a blessing to someone else would open the door to fulfilling the promise?

One month later, I had an appointment with my doctor, and she came into the room with tears in her eyes and said, "Congratulations Jessica, you're pregnant." I could only praise God for hearing my prayer and providing a favor to my womb.

I shared with my doctor, who is also a believer, that I prayed with a group of women, and it was prophetically declared that God would bless my womb. My doctor smiled and said, "Not only are you blessed to have that cluster of sisters, but your baby is also blessed and favored."

The beautiful part of this story is that when I look at our now seven-year-old daughter, God reminds me that delayed never means denied, and He knew what He was doing when He had us face infertility, miscarriages, and doubt. But, on the other side of it all was a miracle who now prays heaven down, serves God at a young age, and brings joy and happiness to many. I don't know if you are in a spiritual or physical season of infertility. You have begged and pleaded with God to bless your womb to open your reproductive system and patent to occupancy; I will tell you that you are not alone and to connect with other sisters who can pray you through. You see, I suffered in silence because I viewed myself as a disgrace for not being able to conceive naturally, but what God did for me at that moment when my cluster of sisters covered me that day no longer allowed my intrusive thinking to forget who God is and what He promised.

May God bless your womb, favored woman! Luke 1:45 says, "You are blessed because you believed that the Lord would do what he said." Whatever you do, do not forget what God said to you. Even if you have to wait a while, know that it will come to pass. I declare that God will send a cluster of women to uphold you just like Aaron and Hur, and that this season of conception will be ordered and directed by God, but, more importantly, soothing and peaceful through prayer, devotion, and sisterhood.

Bio:

Minister Jessica D. Simmons is the youngest daughter of Della Hall. A native of Norfolk, Virginia. Jessica received her education in the Norfolk Public School system, where she earned her advanced diploma from Norview High School in 2005. Upon completing high school, she furthered her education at Tidewater Tech and graduated from the Practical Nursing program in 2007. She served as a Licensed Practical Nurse, offering her medical expertise and knowledge for over ten years. In 2018, Jessica ventured into the field of Human Services and Social work and currently serves as the Program Manager for Team Up Mentoring. Jessica launched her business, Beautiful Blossoms Christian Coaching LLC, in 2018, where her mission is to help women heal healthy and whole. She is married to her devoted husband, Kevin, and they share two children, Cameron and Aubriegh-Rae. Jessica is an example of perseverance and believes that we can grow wherever we are planted.

Chapter 2

Accept Whom God Sends

Rev. Shelia K. Cook

The healing process is necessary as excepting whom God sends to help us. I remember the first time my husband told me he had to go to his family for help concerning me. I initially felt so low, disrespected, and unworthy of the love and devotion he and his family showed me. When dealing with deep wounds, I was a force to be reckoned with; I would suppress and hold on to things while repeatedly masking to cover for my children for years. His making me face my issues was uncharted territory with lots of bursts and anger. The bitter root was being dug up and dealt with. I hadn't realized my husband could see through the smiles that I was in pain from years of rejection and being set aside. It started when we had a party, and it was obvious that some of the people at the party had favorites, and it hurt me to my core. I played it off as usual. However, this time my future husband didn't have it. After taking the kids into the house, he said, "Let's go back to the car and talk it out." We did, and that helped that round.

The next incident was a Christmas gathering, and the gift I purchased was rejected; whew, a flood of pain, memories, and issues began to flood my mind and heart, but again I desperately tried to push it down. Again Mr. made me face them. By this time, we were married. I realized that all these years, I was using shopping as a coping mechanism, so I messed up money during the second quarter of our marriage, after the third year, and lasting until 6th year. My husband went to his mom and his brothers for help concerning me. At first, I was furious with him, embarrassed, and didn't want help. I felt like they were judging me. God calmed that down by allowing us to go on vacation with my husband's family, and casually we all began to talk, and I was able to express the hurt I had suffered for years from family, friends, and so on. Throughout that weekend, I prayed and sought God for complete healing so I could go forth in him whole in the areas I'd been broken in for so many years. That weekend, I learned to accept whom God sends and how He sends them.

My open brokenness helped heal me and our marriage. The mask came off, and I am truly free to be with my family in love on my husband's side. I still have things to work through on my side of the family. The powerful thing is that I learned to let their feelings and opinions be just theirs.

Throughout that whole ordeal, God continued to groom me in ministry. I learned that God would allow us to make it on broken pieces and minister through them. I suffered some hurt by church leaders and friends in the church, but because God had given me the revelation that the phrase "church hurt" is from the pits of hell, I didn't use the hurt to cause me not to go to church. I used it to surrender to God because, at this point, it was his battle, not mine. This is where I found a deeper relationship with God necessary, not just needed. There are things we feel we need but aren't necessary, this is the rubber meets the road, and you meet you. I learned that to live out God's plan for us, we must see how he uses our detours away from him to get us back on track. I tell the reader that all your problems will not disappear once you give your life to God. He gives us the ability to face them with integrity while giving us the endurance to stand through them. I am no longer a fan of suppressing feelings, yet I know it is necessary to use tactics to address certain people with certain issues. I have also learned to be uncut, raw, rare, and original as I move as my authentic self throughout life and ministry.

God gives each of us a cutting edge that no one else has. Because of our experience and personal relationship with him, we can use it to build up his kingdom rather than destroying it by being one of the hurt people, hurt people movement, also known as Me Too. I believe God allowed my pain for its purpose, so I will use my experience to make God's word practical. Pain not surrendered unto God goes uncharted and becomes infected, which in turn poisons your ministry. Get healed, set free, and delivered now in the mighty name of Jesus. You may not think dealing with childhood issues is needed, but believe me, it's necessary. I have been able to face as a woman of God what I couldn't face as a woman still haunted by childhood trauma that wasn't seen as traumatic by others. I thought I was broken and couldn't be fixed. Oh, but God is all I can look at and see damaged goods. He always had his hand on me, just like he has his hand on you; not only did my sister help me heal, but my brothers in love helped me, and my husband helped me heal. Adults need a village, not just children because adults are grown children.

I pray that this chapter helps you truly let God and whom he sends to help you heal.

Bio:

Greetings. I'm Rev. Shelia K. Cook. There is so much I could say, but I will keep it at this; God is a wonder to my soul. How he still chooses us regardless of our faults and flaws. I never imagined being an associate minister at one of the oldest churches in the Seatack community in Virginia Beach, Virginia, Mount Olive Baptist Church, author and co-author. I'm also the founder of God's Love Covers, a virtual ministry birthed out during my come-up season through the scripture 1 Peter 4:8. My prayer is that we can grow together in God as we explore his word together, a family of blood-washed believers. What makes us a strong family is walking in forgiveness and love unmatched by what the world offers us.

Chapter 3

Buried Addiction

By Jarius Hillman

My journey to this point has been difficult, but overall, it has been so good that I wouldn't have it any other way. The reason is that I firmly believe that all things happen for a reason but that all things have a starting point and are a culmination of prior decisions. I didn't know my reason till about last year, but before I elaborate on this, let me say what I had to overcome. This beast was lustful but specifically addicted to porn and masturbation. If I could be deep real quick, the origin of this wasn't when I masturbated for the first time and wasn't even when I was exposed to porn at 3-4 years old. It was when I was born. From starting my healing process and searching for the root, I found out that though others on both sides of my family weren't addicted to porn like I was, they, too, struggled with this issue of lust. With it coming from both sides of family history, it all came in the bundle known as Jarius. This is important because what isn't dealt with is inherited. What my elders didn't heal from or cut off made its way to me, and I had to be the one to break it. This was frustrating because I couldn't understand why this wasn't handled before! Why didn't those who came before me break this? Why did it make its way to me? Why did I have to struggle because of the faults of someone else? These questions burned in my heart, and I had to: 1) Speak them out loud to acknowledge that I recognized them 2) Confront them so I could chop the root. Once I asked these questions, I began to see a lot of the ugly things, but I realized just how much God loved me because He knew me, He saw me, He created me, so He knew all of this was there, yet He kept me, provided, and protected me. It was surreal and opened the door for my private life to change and fully align with God's way.

However, let me not forget all the details in the story because it makes a difference. I explained that I was exposed to porn at a young age, and I remember, even at that time, how my body felt. It was enticing and invigorating! I now know it was because dopamine was released in my 3-4-year-old brain, which gave me a high. This high came whenever I would look at the opposite sex, and it was told by the older men in my life as normal to feel that way looking at a female, but again hindsight is 20/20, right? From there, I grew up trying to sneak looks at porno late at night when I would wake up or stay up on purpose because our internet was slow. I was a good kid but didn't realize that porn made me sneaky and a liar during my young adult and full adult life. I lied about why I was up so late and what I was doing to avoid getting caught. Even to the point that I knew I was caught but didn't care because I wasn't caught in the act. Do you see how distorted this is from a teenager to a young adult and now to a full-grown adult? Not only did it make me a liar and sneaky individual, but this spilled over into my romantic relationships to where at the tender age of 13, I lost my virginity and would've become a teenage parent if the young lady hadn't had a miscarriage. This was a major point in my life, and though I didn't have another incident, I still didn't learn my lesson.

My relationships were still being affected by my inability to overcome lust in my life. It wasn't until I met my mentors, Andre Mason and Jasper Stevens, that I discovered this lust in my life was an attempt to fill a void and self-medicate the thought that I wasn't enough for anyone, especially women. This lie of a thought tormented me for YEARS! This one thought spilled over into my spiritual life, in which I disqualified myself from being available to God even though I was desperate to be close to Him. Those two men and my Pastor, Jeff Whittaker, helped me understand that I wasn't what I was doing, it's not a forever thing, and I could be free! They poured into me and helped me not to deal with symptoms but to get to the core of a thing so I could be better and get out of my way. I'm sure they saw all of this when they prayed or were privy to it still being a struggle, but they loved me through it anyway. Due to their love and willingness, I developed my desire, and that desire for freedom helped me to understand where the root was, how to cut at it, and how to fully recover.

As of today, March 8th, I can even admit that I'm a month and some change porn free! God detoxed me in three days, where I experienced headaches, cold chills, and body aches, then I was fully done. My brothers loved me while knowing where I was but didn't leave me for not listening and heeding. I will forever love and appreciate them because they strengthened me to overcome failures and fall forward. My past is healed. My story is still being written. And my victory is at hand!

Bio:

Jarius Hillman is an author, worship leader, minister, mentor, tech professional, and above all, a Son. Born in the small town of Rustburg, VA, surrounded by farms and cows, he was greatly influenced by mentors and family. The family has shaped him and molded his love for people, compassion for the less fortunate, and selflessness toward those he's around. Although he grew up in a Christian household and was baptized at the age of 8, he didn't develop a relationship with God till he would be on the campus of Old Dominion University singing in the Ebony Impact Gospel Choir. One night after a member bonding event, he was baptized and filled with the Holy Spirit and has since never looked back. From that night, he has made it his mission to spread the Gospel through every gift, talent, and grace so everyone will know Jesus.

Chapter 4

The Bridge

Prophetess Adrianne Demauchet

Ministry has frowned upon mental illness for years due to a lack of understanding. I will try to share my story with you and pray that it will bridge understanding for many in the church world. First, remember that once you encounter a mental health person, they have a back story to the story you see before you. Here are mine as an example. I have been diagnosed with Major depression, bipolar, and anxiety. Later in life, I understood that I also dealt with ADHD. I have learned that when ADHD has been untreated for so long, you will begin dealing with Rejection Sensitive Syndrome. That is when you feel depressed when someone rejects you.

Note: Please encourage mental health people to seek professional help. Some might need medication, and others might need someone to talk to. Whatever it is, please advise them and help them to seek professional help. God uses Doctors too. The enemy might feel some way when taking meds and seeing the doctor, so please reassure them to get the help they need. Some of these illnesses came through generational illness and traumas. I was molested as a kid and raped as an adult, and through it all, many times losing my identity, I didn't know how to love myself and others. Entering the church world, I was pretty messed up. All I ever wanted was to be loved and free.

Mental Health people must attend a place where people Of God believe in deliverance. Many people in the church world are afraid of dealing with deliverance. Jesus delivered many dealing with mental health problems (Matt. 8:16-17). I had to experience many prayer and deliverance moments. Without prayer, fasting, and deliverance, I would still be bound by all those sicknesses. It started when my daughter was hospitalized due to an illness, and two ladies came to pray for us. These two women prayed and laid hands on us. They called out our sickness and began to speak life into us. I was shouting and crying in the hospital room. I was on the floor in tears and didn't know I was getting free at that moment. Note this;

the enemy doesn't want people to know deliverance or self-deliverance. The Bible says in Hosea 4:6(a), "My people are destroyed for lack of knowledge." The enemy would love to keep God's people blinded to the sickness and sin that is kept hidden. That is why we must learn about spirits and what we honestly deal with within ourselves.

Sometimes I didn't even know what I was getting delivered from or why my body would act a certain way during major deliverance. I would get up and be embarrassed and want to run and hide. I even tried to hug and love people afterward and would feel so damaged because the love wasn't shown back. (Many looked down because of what they saw during your deliverance and shunned you for it.) I felt like an outcast for years because I constantly went through deliverance. I didn't understand that I needed it, but then there were times when I didn't. I just needed to understand things fully. Like how to stay free and have grace and mercy like anyone else, knowing that if no one accepts and loves me, GOD DOES. And that it wasn't words that were just being spoken but the truth. What were some things I had to learn on my own? So, remember, teaching is big for someone with a mental health condition. It would be best if you changed how they think to something new instead of allowing them to think and react to what the enemy has been saying for years. Remember that the mental health person has to want to be free to go through the healing process.

With mental health, people need a community that shows them love. They don't need to be frowned upon because the church world doesn't know how to deal with them. Understand that they are sick like anyone else that has a major illness. They need the love of Christ that dwells inside God's people. They didn't need to be pointed out and avoided, but I love them. They don't need someone to say that they are crazy because they fight with that thought in their minds already. Watch out for the words that you say. It would be best to cover yourself because they battle with spirits that fight their minds and behaviors. Cover your eye gates and yourself with the blood of Jesus. Understand that we battle spirits every day within ourselves daily, and they do as well. Move in the spirit of wisdom. Please don't talk about their business with everyone because they may finally be open to talking to you about the situation. Allow them to trust you. I began to pray and ask God how to treat them and how to intercede for them. Keep a community of prayer warriors and intercessors that would quietly pray and fast things off that person.

One more thing, mentally challenged people must learn the Bible and know about fasting. They must come to Bible study and learn about the word of God. They must understand that some things come out by fasting and praying. Once they learn that and desire to be free, they will be free with time. They will be able to experience freedom in their minds and learn how to tame the illness so their real personality can come out.

With these things to know, I hope this has given you peace and understanding of how to deal with mentally challenged people. Please create a manual with places for resources for them in your community. Stay connected to people that work with mental health people. They can instruct you on the different ways to help that person. Keep love and understanding in your heart for them. Discern when the person is not well. Again, with these simple tools, we can come together the way Christ would love us to be.

Bio:

Prophetess Adriannie D. Demauchet is an author, ghostwriter, entrepreneur, and upcoming master coach. She is very creative and a builder. She lives in Houston, Texas, and is a mother of two. She is also the founder and CEO of The ADD Effect LLC. Prophetess Adriannie is known as the Love Nurturer. She has a heart and passion for seeing dreams come to life. She motivates many to chase after their passions and not lose hope. The ADD (which are her initials) Effect comes to ADD to you! She comes to add motivation, love, and drive to gain, overcome, and become that person you always wanted to be.

You can reach The Add Effect on all social media through links.ee/theaddeffect
Email: theaddeffect@yahoo.com
Website: theaddeffect.org

Chapter 5

As I waited Patiently, My Brother Helped Me Heal

Elder Kerry Freeman

In March 2021, my wife and I relocated from Maryland to South Carolina. Once I arrived in South Carolina, I had to process it at the VA Hospital. After completing the blood work, they had me return for an ultrasound of my kidneys, spleen, and liver. The ultrasound revealed spots on my left kidney, and the doctor asked if I had ever been told that I had spots on my left kidney, and I replied no. They had me come back for an MRI of my left kidney, and the results were that I had renal cell cancer in my left kidney. Pastor Luther H. Holmes Jr. and the church prayed for me on the prayer line. I was referred to a kidney specialist at the Augusta University Medical Center in Georgia. The doctor informed me that the cancer was in the kidney and that they would have to remove my left kidney. When I got that news from the doctor, my heart started racing as I listened to the doctor's prognosis. I didn't ever think that I could be diagnosed with cancer.

But then I remembered how when I had pneumonia in 2012, it turned into double pneumonia and viral pneumonia. The doctor said there was nothing he could do for me. The doctor told me I needed to see a lung specialist. One of the deacons called me and prayed with me, and in that prayer, God told me I was healed. I went to see the lung specialist and had a test run, and they told me to come back in three days for the test results. In three days, I returned to the lung specialist to receive the results: all tests were negative. God had healed me, and I knew if he had done it before, he could bring me through again.

While visiting my mom in Virginia, Pastor Bruce E. Hughes prayed for me at the altar at church. My wife and my daughter prayed for me in my home. Minister Lonnie Clark drove my wife and me to the Georgia hospital to have the surgery. On July 16th, 2021, I had successful surgery to remove my left kidney. Pastor Luther H. Holmes Jr. visited the hospital that evening following surgery and prayed for me. The nurse at the Augusta University Medical Center in Georgia told me I was lucky they found kidney cancer early because it is usually not found until it is too late and you die from it. I told the nurse it was not luck, but God had them find the kidney cancer to preserve my life because I belong to God. After a three-day stay in the hospital, I was released, and Minister Clark picked my wife and me up from the hospital and drove us back to SC. The doctor told me I would need about two months to recover, so I could not do manual work. During recovery, I had other medical conditions flare up due to the trauma from the surgery removing my left kidney. I developed a hydrosol in my groin that left me in severe pain and unable to sit without a cushion under me. I also had a hernia flare-up in my lower abdomen, which caused excruciating pain.

While home recovering, I had scheduled to have my kitchen floor replaced and had to have the kitchen table removed so the work could be done. I called Minister Clark, who came over and moved the table for me. Elder Stephen Harris called and asked if he could do anything for me, and I told him my grass needed cutting. Elder Harris came to my house, mowed my grass, and edged around the house and sidewalk. Elder Dexter Johnson called me and asked if I needed anything, and

I told him I had a taste for some fish. Eder Johnson came to my house and brought some fresh fish from the fish market. I was in so much pain that I could not bend down. After showering daily, my wife had to dry me off and dress me. I thank God for my wife, who was right by my side every day, to help me along the way. My daughter Keri and my grandson Ethan visited and brought me fruits. My grandson Ethan saw me walking to the bathroom, struggling to make it, and said, "Why don't you use that walking cane you have?" He went into the garage and got the old cane from when my knee was operated on. Out of the mouth of babes as it took my grandson Ethan to point out that I needed to use my walking cane.

My son Kerry Jr. and grandsons Kerry III and Kordell visited, and my son repaired the toilet in my home for me. Now that the kitchen floor was complete, I needed the kitchen table back in place. I called Minister Haywood Dawkins, and he came over, put the table back into the kitchen, and moved my sofas for me in the living room. After about a month into my recovery, I could go back to church, but my wife had to drive me, and I could only wear loose sweatpants as I still had sores in my stomach. I wanted to be in the church because the church is our hospital. I wouldn't say I liked that I could not wear my nice suits, but I was glad to be in the service. When your brother is in need, prayer is good, and prayer works, but there are physical needs that your brother needs. My brothers not only just prayed for me, but they also met my physical needs while I was down. My brothers prayed for me and met my physical needs by moving furniture in my house, mowing my lawn, and bringing me food. After two months of recovery, I returned to my old self, going to church, walking through the neighborhood with my wife, playing with my grandsons, driving my truck, and playing golf again. I thank God for all he has done for my brothers and me in helping me heal.

Bio:

I was born in Virginia Beach, Va., on November 10th, 1967. After graduating from High School in 1986, I went to college in North Carolina. After attending Johnson C. Smith University in Charlotte, NC, for a year, I transferred to Norfolk State University. While attending College in Virginia, I married, and my daughter was born in 1988. After two years of college in Virginia, I dropped out and enlisted in the US Army. After attending Basic Training at Fort Sill, Oklahoma, I was shipped to my first duty station in Germany. While in Germany, my son was born in 1991. In 1996 while stationed in Ft Lewis, Washington, I gave my life to Christ. I returned to college, attended Thomas Edison State College, and earned my BA in Business Administration in 2007. After serving in the US Army for 20 years and numerous deployments to Saudi Arabia, Korea, Egypt, Cuba, and Norway, I retired in 2010. While working for the government in Indiana in 2012, I was called to preach. I returned to Liberty University and earned my BA in Religion in 2015. While working as a government contractor in South Carolina and serving faithfully as a Minister, I was ordained as an Elder in 2017. After two years of separation, I was divorced in 2018. While working as a government contractor in Maryland, I married again in 2018 to my lovely wife, Felicia Freeman. We relocated to South Carolina to be around our four grandsons in 2021. I serve at Ecclesia COGIC in Columbia, SC., as an Elder, Sunday School Teacher, and Mission Department President.

Chapter 6

Not My Own

Paige Edmonds

When asked to write this chapter, I was nervous. I could think of a sister that helped me heal. I was a hold child (by default) who was taught the importance of independence. Friends, I had but kept at arm's length, thinking they couldn't handle the inner workings of who I was or the shame I carried—close family members who saw one thing without seeking understanding.

Mentors who reached out required me to make the first move. Yes, I had people there, but I felt like I healed myself through the help of God.

All I could depend on was me. If something went wrong, I only had myself to blame. If something didn't get done, it was on me. I placed life responsibilities on myself that were never designed for one person to carry; I just thought I had to.

You may be reading this thinking, Man, she is self-centered, but that can't be further from the truth. To fully understand, let's start from the beginning.

I was born to the world's best parents, Ted and Kim Hines. Life overall was pretty good! We lived in a beautiful home with many rooms and bathrooms. I attended private school until middle school, then attended one of the top high schools in the area, Eleanor Roosevelt High School. My parents allowed me to do whatever I thought I wanted. You name it: from dancing to track to guitar lessons, I tried it. I dined at the finest restaurant the DMV had to offer. I traveled to Aruba, Africa, London, the Bahamas, and a few states by plane and car. I was exposed to culture and the arts through Broadway and local theater. Day trips to New York and road trips to Florida and Myrtle Beach were a part of every summer adventure. A lot, I know! Spoiled, nope, just dearly loved. Despite all this and more, I was struggling secretly. I didn't mention before that my siblings passed away, causing me to become the only child. Some question why I could miss something I never honestly had the chance to experience.

I never met my sister, Ashley, but I know she was born. My time with my little brother Jason was short, but I remember my parents bringing him home. Filling the void of something you didn't fully experience is possible. Trust me; it's very likely.

After losing my brother, my mother was diagnosed with a fatal brain tumor. According to a few doctors' reports, the operation wasn't an option because of the tumor's placement. The likelihood of her dying on the table was too high. So, at three, I was taught the importance of independence. Yes, that is a massive lesson for someone so young, but preparation takes precedence when death is at the door. I learned I was responsible for feeding myself in the morning in case Daddy overslept. I learned how to entertain myself by turning on my television and entering a Barney tape into the VCR.

My independence was born out of necessity. Even though the Lord delivered my mother, who is still with us today (insert praise), those lessons of self-dependence never left.

With so much loss and trials, I decided to be all things to my parents. A burden pressed upon me by one but myself, I felt that because I was the last man standing, it was my responsibility to ensure our parents were good. With all that my parents went through and overcame, I felt like their previous child that it was on me. So, I became the tomboy my father never had by playing sports, mainly running track, just like him. I became a ballerina and travel buddy to my mom. As the Bible says, I became all things to all men. To produce a level of perfection only found in fairy tales and movies. To be the perfect daughter, the best track runner, the cutest dancer, to be without spot or wrinkle until I wasn't.

My innocence was taken from me. I was molested for years. I carried the shame of my molesters' actions thinking it was my own. Carrying it alone because I felt I had to. How could the perfect daughter not be perfect anymore? How can the last child standing be damaged goods? I had let my siblings down. I had left myself, and my parents did. How could I tell them? They had endured so much already; I couldn't add to their pain. I can't add to their troubles. I eat it and continue to do my assignment., alone.

I hope you are seeing this unhealthy pattern I created for myself. Responsibility to hold it all together without the assistance of others was my thing. I thought it was the level of independence I needed to survive, to make it. I can't depend on someone because they could leave. Leave like my siblings before I could try developing a relationship with them. I was almost left like my mother due to illness or betraying my trust like the young man who molested me. The art of developing healthy relationships was lost on me, causing me to keep everyone at arm's length. I trusted no one and left at first sight of trouble.

But then I went to college.

I ran to one of the only two schools to accept me, Saint Augustine's University in Raleigh, North Carolina. During my parents' weekend, a lady gave my father a flyer to attend church on Sunday. That church would become my place of transformation. I met a young lady by the name of Kenya Wagner. She became my friend through my college church events, choir rehearsals, bible studies, and late-night conversations. Through time, she evolved into my sister! I never made a problem making friends; I struggled to keep them, but Kenya was different. She accepted me without judgment as I found my way to Christ. Her support and consistent encouragement helped my development during my college years. God graced me with a few women who covered me during this season, Keesha White (my college mom).

My heart was open to help from a sister. For the first time, I didn't feel the need to do it alone. It started with my relationship with God. Allowing him in allowed me to see how help didn't make you weak but your strength to acknowledge your shortcomings to become better. One scripture that was hard to accept was in your WEAKNESS; HIS strength is made perfect. After this turning point, I experienced many weak moments, but the women listed made it more accessible.

Post-college was an exciting season. I was in my first "saved" relationship that didn't meet my expectations. I gained a lasting relationship with First Lady Hope McMillian through that relationship. She helped me heal. She prayed with and for me and told me the truth even when it was hard to hear. She held me accountable and pushed me toward healing.

Sada Messiah helped me heal. I was introduced to her through a mutual friend. She was a young wife whom God used to prepare me for today. She spoke life to me, challenged my perspectives, and encouraged a deeper relationship with God. Through her authenticity and genuine spirit, she helped me heal.

After being found by my husband, I moved to a new state with new rules and people. Terrified and worried my true self wouldn't be accepted in a consecutive area, my sister-in-love, Maria Edmonds, and mother-in-love, Debra Edmonds, helped me heal. They covered me in situations my complex outspoken self caused. They encouraged me when life knocked the air out of my lungs. I am forever grateful for the continued love and support my in-laws provide me. Because they accepted the authentic version of myself, they are helping me heal!

This situation has been a struggle, and I am still working through it with the help of my sister Nakesha and JaNyta. Nakesha is showing me the importance of maintaining who you are, even in elevation, keeping the spice that makes me the best version of myself. She encourages me to keep evolving and allowing God to direct me. And JaNtya, my co-worker turned confidant turned sister, is fighting with me daily. Her direct, honest, yet loving words continue to shine a light on flaws and greatness. They are helping me heal!

In conclusion, I compare my life to the Walking in the Sand story. I felt I endured every heartbreak, trial, and hardship for years. I thought it was never seen, even in a room full of people. I felt that God alone made it to where I am today. But just like the poem said, when I look back and only see one set of footsteps, it was because my sisters (and mothers) were helping me heal.

Bio:

Paige A. Edmonds, M.A. is known for her one-of-a-kind vivacious personality and spirit; she is a woman of prayer that loves God and His people. Born August 1st to Assistant Pastor Booker T. Hines Jr and Evang. Kimberly Hines it was clear at a young age that Paige was wise beyond her years and anointed by God.

She met the love of her life, Pastor Frederick M. Edmonds, Sr, at a young adult conference in Maryland and was engaged within seven months of meeting! God has blessed them with three beautiful children from this union, Frederick Jr, Solomon, and Princess Adelle.

One of her greatest joys is serving alongside her husband in ministry at Bethlehem Church of God Christ, where she serves as First Lady.

Chapter 7

Shed to Soar

Prophetess Ronjeanna Harris

There is always a moment to ponder your place of wholeness. Ask the question of whether I overcame that. Healing is beautiful, and the discovery is simply a breathtaking encounter. We get to see the story unfold with every odd conquered. This is truly a very realistic experience. The master creator created our life to operate in abundance. I know all too well about this. For a long time, I kept focusing on the ugly of the shedding but didn't fully capture the beauty of shedding. I didn't understand how vital it was to my healing and effective elevation. But then, I grasped the understanding. It was extraordinary. The breathing intake for the moments of rising above the surface healing helps me heal more efficiently.

I had all that unnecessary pressure still packed away because there was more shedding to encounter successfully. I started feeling and looking lighter.

How do you gather knowledge without missing the moment? There must be an in-depth surrender to God's every plan. God sees even the most attempted hidden layers. God designed us so he knows his architect's original form, a tampered edition of us. Our earthly journeys and jobs require us to operate and function from a healed place. God is so amazing to even consider and prepare for our self-afflicted interruptions. One of my biggest problems was second-guessing who I was in God. Even in that, it opens doors for the enemy to have a field day in my life. This is why the scripture "Be ye transformed by the renewing of your mind" (Bible KJV) is so important. This scripture is imperative in proper healing because it helps shut down the plan of the enemy's agenda on our life. God was and still is a major part of my healing. I love how special people and moments were contributors to my healing process. I didn't want it, but I was still considered for the purpose. I want the person reading this to know that you are considered for God's glory and plan for your life. Lift your head and embrace your healing.

It is great when healing truly takes place. Your conversations are different. You give people hope because you have overcome and healed for future assignments to be successful. My husband of 18 years, Floyd Harris, is also a huge part of my healing. He never stops being consistent in being a provider and protector as King of the home. He didn't let life stop him from doing what was right for his family. I experienced several failed relationships before him. There was a demonstration of determination even when tuff times came. My husband's strength is so amazing to me. He is an example that there are still great men out there. God's hand picks us to be one. This helped my shedding and stopped me from blocking walls in my personal space in my home when moments of disagreement were experienced. The bible even states that we can agree to disagree. Our views weren't always the same, but that did not mean that healthy discussions couldn't be had to come to an agreed solution. I understand that God still ordained our union even in touch times. Also, as healing occurred properly, we still evolved in learning from each other more in-depth. We have survived what would have made some fold and given in. God knew that I needed structure, and my husband needed realism. Our blended family needed to see this demonstration.

Shedding all of life's unassigned weights was an emergency operation that required multiple surgical intakes. Remember, the layers did not build up overnight. That said, a healthy plan of action is not needed because this helps guide us to heal.

We must set healing goals like those for other areas of our life. Getting to the point of enough is enough of the despair cycles was a big driving agent for me. I no longer want to make decisions or choices from an unhealed place. This made me push the sternness of accountability to me first be guided by God almighty properly.

How do you keep the process of healing a continuous success? Let me share some wholesome nuggets to encourage the amazing person to read this. First is always acknowledgment of the wounded and hurt place within. Align with the step needed to begin the process and the levels it will take. Seek God frequently for guidance and insight. Be honest with yourself. After all, you owe your chosen hood the opportunity to flourish prominently. Set boundaries to complete all parts involved in the healing process. Keep yourself and all participants accountable to master the goals that align with the design of your healing. Give hope another chance to reign in your life. Be at peace with your past. That is a huge must for several areas of your life. Tear down the walls of the setback. Set your thoughts on the things above. (Colossians 3:2 The Bible KJV) Keep your heart postured to God so the cares of life won't create a punctured impact. Many say pick up the pieces, but I suggest you allow God to be the potter for what shatter you may have experienced. Allow your past to be a lesson and not view it as a failure. Conquer the challenges and make time to shed effectively by releasing all the things that have no contribution to your healing journey. Pray frequently and be intentional when doing so. Always remember that someone may need the same guidance you had to get; let that be another reason to heal successfully.

Shed to soar; there are new garments awaiting you. God is waiting on you to complete the process, so be positioned to obtain your new attire. Healing is your portion, and you deserve to live a healed life. Be Encouraged!

Bio:

Ronjeanna Harris is a God-fearing and chosen ordained Evangelist, affirmed Prophet, and Intercessor. Ronjeanna is a devoted wife, mother of six, and grandmother of two. Ronjeanna is an LPN with over 20 yrs. Skill and experience in healthcare. This game-changer is the proud owner of Just Jeanna's Skin Care LLC. Natural Product Creator & Formulator was launched as a company in 2018 after much prayer, research, and preparation. After just two years in business, Just Jeanna's Skin Care LLC got approved to be in the Walmart marketplace in 2020. Ronjeanna is a 7 x Amazon # 1 best seller Author, LPN, and award-winning Certified Wellness Coach with over 20 years of experience and skill in the healthcare industry. Just Jeanna's Skin Care LLC offers a host of local, national, and international services. This trailblazer, in May 2020, started her non-profit organization, Jeanna's iFeed, doing what she loves: being a servant. Jeanna's IFeed is a multi-award-winning non-profit known for its esteemed consistency of serving the communities in the Hampton Roads and Eastern Shore of VA. Kingdom Solutionist Coaching & Mentoring Services was born in 2021. Community serving and giving back is an honor and passion for Ronjeanna. Ronjeanna is a proud member of Cornerstone City Refuge Global Alliance (The New City Church of VA) under the Leadership of Apostle Dannie & Pastor Rebecca Ducksworth, serving as Evangelist. Providing natural wellness solutions is Ronjeanna's mission to stand by.

FB, IG, YouTube and LinkedIn
Just Jeanna's Skin Care

FB & IG
Jeanna's feed

Online Kingdom Health Wellness School

Epilogue

Destiny Helpers

by Dr. Chavon Anette

My Sister and My Brother Helped Me Heal! I cannot believe a yes in 2021 would become what it is today. A collaboration first for women has opened to both men and women. The reality is that life's challenges did not end for any co-author in 2022. I have seen these women and men remain resilient and faithful to a consistent God as new challenges arise.

My sister and brother helped me heal was never an anthology to show the arrival of a person. It was an opportunity to celebrate what every individual could overcome, and the people God sent on their path to do just that.

If you are reading this book, I understand it is because you have found yourself in dark seasons in the past, or maybe something is present before you know. I pray that this book has been a source of healing and hope for you. One never knows when another storm will come, but we learn how to handle the next last storm better.

Allow God to bring the destiny helpers in your life. Share your story. Listen to the wisdom of those who love you. Trust God's word concerning your life. Embrace and hold on to the community that God has placed around you. The strength in numbers overrides the trials that seem too heavy to bear.

It's okay that life is not perfect because you serve the perfect God. It's okay to cry because God loves wiping away your tears. God is there to be your help and to send you help.

Healing is a process that is not pretty, but it's worth it. Every story that you have read has been one that took time and attention. Make time to heal. Give attention to your mental, emotional, and psychological state. The best version of you is the healed version of you. Many ignore the signs of distress, which takes a complete breakdown before the journey starts. Don't allow that to be your story. Create the boundary, inform a friend, connect with the community, seek therapy, and pray so you can heal.

The world needs what's in you. However, you cannot give anyone the best of who you are in a broken state. It does not mean perfection is required, but it does mean that healing should be in progress after injury. If not, you are more dangerous to others than they are to you.

It's hard, but you can do this! Heal and live life to the fullest. God has a plan for your life, and it's hard to see that in the thick of it. Nevertheless, God is the God who specializes in turning chaos and pain into a glorious victory.

Visionary Bio

First and foremost, Dr. Chavon Anette is a daughter of God! She is a Prophetess as well. She is the CEO of Purpose Unwrapped, LLC and non-profit Power and Grace Leaders, Inc. Dr. Chavon is affectionately known as the Fire Leadership Coach. God has called her to make an impact in ministry and the marketplace.

She is currently in school working toward a Doctorate in Education in Chrisitan Leadership from Liberty University to be completed in May 2024. While on that journey, God saw fit for her to allow her the esteemed honor of receiving an honorary doctorate degree for Divinity In February 2023 for the work she already does on Earth from The School of Great Commission Bible College.

As the Fire Leadership Coach, She marries practical and spiritual tools to empower and equip kingdom people to lead in the world. She is also a mentor to many.

She balances entrepreneurship, ministry, and employment as the Student Success Manager at Regent University. She enjoys creating experiences for holistic transformation, so she annually hosts two significant events: Fanning the Flame

Experience, Power and Grace Leaders Awards Gala, and the Powerhouse Leaders Conference.

She is also a transformational speaker and minister of the gospel who speaks with great passion in a way that empowers and challenges her listeners. She has been featured as a speaker on ABC News, TCT Today, Norfolk State University, Virginia Wesleyan University, and at conferences and other events such as the globally recognized Comeback Champion Summit, Sister Leads Conference, and more.

Dr. Chavon has published four books that are available on Amazon, and she has been a part of seven anthologies. From Pain to Purpose was her first solo project that became an Amazon #1 Bestselling book. She is the visionary of volumes of My Sister Helped Me Heal Anthology and My Brother Helped Me Heal, an Amazon #1 Bestselling Anthology movement.

Chavon Anette was the 2021 Servant Leader of the Year Award Recipient from ACHI Magazine.

www.ingramcontent.com/pod-product-compliance
Lightning Source LLC
Chambersburg PA
CBHW060034180426
43196CB00045B/2684